Memoirs of Childhood and Youth

Memoirs of
Childhood and Youth

⧗

Albert Schweitzer

Translated by
Kurt Bergel *and* Alice R. Bergel

Syracuse University Press

First Syracuse University Press Edition 1997
97 98 99 00 01 02   6 5 4 3 2 1

Frontispiece: Albert Schweitzer and child. Photograph by N. Fine. Courtesy of *The Courier.*

The publication of this book was assisted by a generous grant from the William Fleming Educational Fund.

The translators gratefully acknowledge the help they received from Peter Bergel and Linda Gruver.

This translation is based on the original German edition by C. H. Beck'sche Verlagsbuchhandlung, München 1924.

The paper used in this publication meets the minimum requirements of American National Standard for Information Sciences—Permanence of Paper for Printed Library Materials, ANSI 39.48. ∞™

Library of Congress Cataloging-in-Publication Data
Schweitzer, Albert, 1875–1965.
[Aus meiner Kindheit und Jugendzeit. English]
Memoirs of childhood and youth / Albert Schweitzer ; translated by Kurt Bergel and Alice R. Bergel.—1st Syracuse University Press ed.
p. cm.
ISBN 0-8156-0446-7 (alk. paper)
1. Schweitzer, Albert, 1875–1965—Childhood and youth.
2. Missionaries, Medical—Gabon—Biography. 3. Theologians—
Europe—Biography. 4. Musicians—Europe—Biography.
5. France—Biography.
I. Bergel, Kurt. II. Bergel, Alice R. III. Title.
CT1018.S45A3 1997
610'.92—dc21
[B]   96–49619

⧗

While I was packing my things (for my second stay in
Africa in 1924), I wrote down memories of my childhood and youth as a result of a get-together with my
friend, Dr. O. Pfister, the well-known Zürich psycho-
analyst. Early in the summer of 1923, while traveling
across Switzerland from west to east, I used a stopover
of two hours to visit him. He offered me refreshments
and gave me the chance to stretch my tired limbs. At
the same time, he urged me to tell him some incidents
of my childhood just as they would come into my
mind. He wanted to publish them in a young people's
magazine. Later he sent me what he had taken down
in shorthand in those two hours. I asked him not to
publish it but to leave it to me to complete. Shortly
before my departure for Africa, on a Sunday afternoon,
while it was raining and snowing, I wrote down as a

conclusion to what I had told him some thoughts which moved me as I looked back upon my youth.

Albert Schweitzer

Out of My Life and Thought (New York, 1990), 206.

Memoirs of Childhood and Youth

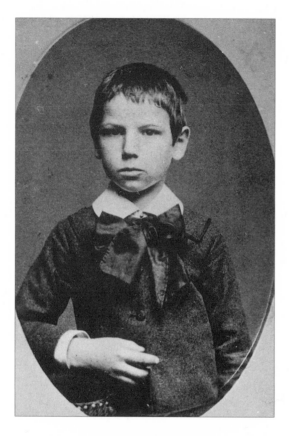

Albert Schweitzer at age nine. Courtesy of the Albert Schweitzer Center and Syracuse University Library.

Out of My Childhood and Youth

I was born on January 14, 1875, in little Kaysersberg in Upper Alsace in the house with the turret, on the left side as you leave town. My father was the pastor and teacher of the small Protestant congregation of Kaysersberg, which was mainly Catholic. When Alsace became French, the small vicarage ceased to exist. The little house with the turret has now become the police station. I was the second child, following a sister who was my elder by a year.

The famous medieval preacher Geiler von Kaysersberg (1445–1510), who used to give sermons at Strasbourg Cathedral, took his name from this town. Born in Schaffhausen in Switzerland, he grew up in the house of his grandfather in Kaysersberg after the death of his father.

The vintage of 1875 was excellent. As a boy I took great pride in having been born in Geiler von

The house where Albert Schweitzer was born in Kaysersberg, Alsace. Courtesy of the Albert Schweitzer Center and Syracuse University Library.

Kaysersberg's hometown in a year famous for its wines.

Half a year after my birth, my father moved to Günsbach in the Münster Valley to be its pastor. My mother hailed from this region; she was the daughter of Pastor Schillinger in Mühlbach, farther back in the valley. When we came to Günsbach, I was a very weak child. On the day my father was inaugurated as pastor, my mother decked me out as best she could in a little white dress with colored ribbons. Despite her efforts none of the neighboring pastors' wives who had come for the celebration dared compliment her on the scrawny baby with the little yellow face. They took refuge in embarrassed commonplaces. At that point my mother—she often told me this—could no longer control herself: she fled with me to the bedroom and shed hot tears over me. At one time they even thought I was dead, but the milk of neighbor Leopold's cow and the good Günsbach air worked wonders on me. From my second year on, I became healthy and grew up a strong boy. In the parsonage of Günsbach I spent a happy childhood with three sisters and a brother. A sixth child, a girl named Emma, was taken from my parents by an early death.

Albert Schweitzer (right) *at the age of five with his sisters. Courtesy of Syracuse University Library.*

My earliest recollection is of seeing the Devil. When I was three or four years old, I was allowed to go along to church every Sunday. I looked forward to that all week. I still feel our maid's cotton glove on my lips when she put her hand over my mouth to stifle my yawn or when I sang along too loud. Every Sunday I saw in a shiny frame up on the side of the organ a shaggy face moving back and forth and looking down into the church. It became visible when the organ was played and the singing began, disappeared as my father prayed at the altar, returned with the organ playing and singing, disappeared once again when my father was preaching and later reappeared once more with organ playing and singing. "This is the Devil looking into the church," I told myself. "When your father preaches the word of God, he has to make himself scarce." This theology, which I experienced every Sunday, shaped my childlike piety. Only much later, when I had been going to school for quite some time, did it become clear to me that the shaggy face which so strangely appeared and disappeared was that of Father Iltis, the organist. It appeared in a mirror which was mounted on the organ so the organist could see when my father stepped to the altar or went up to the pulpit.

Another event I remember from my earliest child-hood is the moment when I felt consciously ashamed of myself for the first time. I was still wearing a little skirt and was sitting on a small stool in the yard while my father was busying himself about the beehives in the garden. Soon, a pretty little creature landed on my hand. I was delighted to watch it crawling back and forth. But suddenly I began to scream. The little crea-ture was a bee, which was justifiably angry that the pastor was taking the full honeycombs from the bee-hive. In revenge it stung the pastor's little son. Upon my screams the whole household came rushing out. Everyone commiserated with me. The maid took me in her arms and tried to console me with kisses. My mother reproached my father for working at the bee-hives without first putting me in a safe place. Since my misfortune had made me so interesting, I kept crying with satisfaction until I suddenly became aware that I was shedding tears without feeling pain any longer. My conscience told me to stop now; but in order to remain the center of attention, I continued my lamentation and went on accepting consolations which I no longer needed. In doing so I felt so despica-ble that I was unhappy for days. How often has the memory of this experience restrained me when, as a grown-up, I felt tempted to make a fuss about something that happened to me.

The terror of my early childhood was the sacristan and gravedigger Jägle. On Sunday mornings after the first ringing of the bells, he came to the parsonage to pick up the numbers of the hymns that were to be sung and the baptismal vessels. He used to touch my forehead and say, "The horns are growing." I worried about the horns because I had rather pronounced bumps on my forehead. These caused me a great deal of anxiety since I had seen in the Bible a picture of Moses with horns. I don't know how the sacristan found out about my worries, but he did know them and he fueled them. When he wiped his feet in front of the door before ringing the doorbell on Sundays, I felt like running away. But he had me in his power as the snake does the rabbit. I could not help but face him, feel his hand on my forehead and accept his damning pronouncement. After having carried the anguish about with me for a year or so, I brought Moses' horns up in a conversation with my father and learned from him that Moses had been the only human who ever had horns. Therefore, I had nothing more to fear.

When the sacristan noticed that I was escaping him, he devised something new. He talked to me about soldiering. "Now we are Prussian," he would say, "and with the Prussians everybody has to be a soldier. And the soldiers wear iron uniforms. In a few years you must be fitted with an iron uniform by the blacksmith up the street." From then on I sought every opportunity to stop in front of the blacksmith's shop and see whether some soldier was coming to be fitted for such a uniform. But only horses and donkeys showed up to be shod. On a later occasion, as my mother and I were looking at a picture of a cuirassier, I asked her about the iron uniforms of soldiers. To my relief I found out that ordinary soldiers wore uniforms made of cloth and that I would be a common soldier.

The sacristan, an old soldier who had fought in the Crimean War, was one of those dry jokers of whom there has never been a lack in Günsbach. He wanted to teach me how to take a joke. But he was somewhat too hard a taskmaster for me. As sacristan and gravedigger he was extremely dignified. He strode through the church with a majestic bearing, but otherwise he was known for being a bit odd. One morning in the haying season he was about to go off to the fields with a rake when a man stopped him to report the death of his father and to order a grave dug. The sacristan reacted with the words, "Why, anybody could come along and say that his father had died." Once we passed by his house on a Sunday evening in midsummer. He came up to my father almost in tears and confided to him the story of his calf. He had raised a fine calf which followed him around like a dog. In the beginning of the summer, he had taken it out to graze in the hills and that Sunday he had gone to visit it. The calf did not recognize him. It acted as if he were a man like any other. This ingratitude hurt him deeply. The calf was not allowed back into its stable. He sold it right away.

I did not look forward to school. When, on a beautiful October day, my father first put the slate under my arm and took me to the teacher, I cried all the way. I had an inkling that this meant the end of my dreaming and my glorious freedom. Since then, I have never allowed my expectations to be dazzled by the beautiful aura which clothes the new. I have always stepped into the unknown without illusions.

The first visit of the school inspector made a deep impression on me. This was not just because the teach-

The village of Günsbach, Upper Alsace, where Schweitzer spent his childhood. Courtesy of the Albert Schweitzer Center and Syracuse University Library.

er's hands trembled with excitement as she offered him the class register, and Father Iltis—who ordinarily looked so stern—kept smiling and bowing. No, what moved me so deeply was that I saw for the first time, face to face, a man who had written a book. It was his name—he was called Steinert—which appeared on the covers of the yellow intermediate reader and the green upper grade one. And now I saw before me in the flesh the author of these two books, which to me came right after the Bible. He did not look imposing. He was short, bald, had a red nose and a little pot-belly and was wedged in a gray suit. To me, though, he wore a halo, for he was a man who had written a book! It seemed incomprehensible to me that the school master and mistress were talking with him as with an ordinary mortal.

That first meeting with a writer of books was soon followed by a second even more significant experience. Mausche, a Jew from a neighboring village, who dealt in cattle and land, occasionally passed through Günsbach with his donkey cart. Since there were then no Jews living in our village, this was an event for the local boys each time. They ran after him and made fun of him. In order to advertise that I was beginning to feel grown-up, I felt compelled to join in one day, even though I did not really know what it was all about. So I followed him and his donkey with the other boys, shouting "Mausche, Mausche!" like them. The most courageous of us folded the corner of their apron or their jacket to look like a pig's ear and jumped with it to him as close as possible. In this manner we pursued him beyond the village down to the bridge. Mausche, however, with his freckles and his gray beard, continued on his way as unperturbed as his donkey. Only now and then did he turn around and look at us with an embarrassed, good-natured smile. This smile overwhelmed me. From Mausche I learned for the first time what it means to be silent in the face of persecution. He became a great educator for me. From that time on, I used to greet him respectfully. Later, as a high school student, I got accustomed to shaking hands with him and accompanying him a little way. But he never knew what he meant to me. There was a rumor that he was a usurer and unscrupulous real estate shark. I never investigated that. To me he remains Mausche with the forgiving smile, who even now forces me to be patient when I feel like fuming and raging.

I did not look for fights, but I loved to match bodily strength with others in friendly scuffles. One day on my way home from school, I wrestled with George Nitschelm—he now rests beneath the earth—who was taller and was considered stronger than I, and I beat him. As he was lying under me, he hissed, "Darn it, if I got soup with meat twice a week as you do, I would be as strong as you are!" Shaken by this outcome of the game, I staggered home. George Nitschelm had expressed with shocking clarity what I had already come to feel on other occasions. The village boys did not fully accept me as one of their own. To them I was one who was better off than they, the parson's son, the gentleman's boy. I suffered because of this, for I did not want to be different from them or to be better off. The meat soup became loathsome to me. Whenever it was steaming on the table, I heard George Nitschelm's voice.

From then on I anxiously tried not to distinguish myself from the others in any way. For the winter I had been given an overcoat made out of an old one of my father's. But no village boy wore an overcoat. When the tailor tried it on me and said, "My goodness, Albert, you will soon be a monsieur!" I could hardly

Schweitzer, wearing a noticeable collar (second row, center),
with his school class. Courtesy of Syracuse University Library.

hold back my tears. On the day I was to wear it for the first time—it was on a Sunday morning for church—I refused. There ensued an ugly scene. My father slapped my face. To no avail. They had to take me along without the overcoat. After that each time I was supposed to wear the coat, the same thing happened. How many blows I received on account of that piece of clothing! But I stood my ground.

That same winter my mother took me with her to Strasbourg to visit an elderly relative. On that occasion she wanted to buy me a cap. In a fine store they had me try on a few. In the end, my mother and the saleswoman settled for a nice sailor's cap, which I was to wear immediately. But they had reckoned without their host. The cap was unacceptable to me because none of the village boys wore a sailor's cap. When they urged me to take it or another of the ones I had tried on, I made such a scene that everyone in the store rushed up to me. "Well, what kind of cap do you want, you silly boy?" the saleswoman snapped. "I don't want any of your new-fangled ones, I want one like the ones the village boys wear." So they sent a salesgirl to get me a brown cap that could be pulled down over the ears, from the unsalable stock. Beaming with joy, I put it on while my poor mother had to endure a few "nice" remarks and scornful glances on account of her oaf.

It pained me that she felt ashamed before the city folk because of me. Still, she did not scold me. She must have had an inkling that something serious lay behind my behavior.

This hard struggle continued as long as I attended the village school and embittered not only my life but also that of my father. I wanted to wear mittens exclusively because the village boys did not wear any other kind of glove. On weekdays I wanted to walk only in clogs because they wore leather shoes only on Sundays. Every visitor who came rekindled the conflict, for I was supposed to present myself in clothes "befitting our social position." While at home, I gave in to all demands; but whenever I was told to go for a walk with the visitor dressed as a "gentleman's boy," I became again the obstreperous fellow who infuriated his father—the courageous hero who endured being slapped and locked up in the cellar. Nevertheless, I suffered badly from rebelling against my parents. My sister Louise, who was a year older than I, understood what I was going through and was touchingly sympathetic. The village boys did not know the cross I bore because of them. They coolly accepted all my efforts not to differ from them, but would, when the least quarrel occurred, wound me again with the terrible words "gentleman's boy."

At the beginning of my school years, I had to cope with one of the hardest lessons that life teaches us—a friend betrayed me. This is how it happened. When I first heard the word "cripple," I did not know what it meant. It seemed to me to express a particularly strong dislike. One newly arrived teacher, Miss Goguel, had not yet earned my favor, so I bestowed the mysterious word upon her. When I was guarding the cows with my best friend, I confided to him in a secretive manner, "The teacher is a cripple, but don't you tell anybody!" He promised.

On the way to school a short time afterwards, we had a falling out. Then he whispered to me on the stairs, "O.K., I'm going to tell the teacher that you called her a cripple." I did not take the threat seriously, for I did not think such betrayal possible. But during the break he really did go up to the teacher's desk and announced, "Miss, Albert said that you are a cripple." Nothing came of it for the teacher did not understand what the statement was supposed to mean. I, however, could not grasp the horror of it. This first experience of betrayal smashed to pieces everything that I had thought and expected of life. It took me weeks to get over the shock. I had lost my innocence about life. I bore within me the painful wound which life inflicts on us all and which it reopens again and again with new blows. Some of the blows I have received since then were harder than that first one, but none has hurt more.

Even before I started school, my father had begun to instruct me in music on an old square piano. I did not play much sheet music. Rather, it was my delight to improvise and play songs and chorale melodies with accompaniments of my own invention. When the teacher in singing class repeatedly played the chorale one note at a time without accompaniment, I thought it lacked beauty, so I asked her during the break why she didn't play it correctly with accompaniment. In my zeal I sat down at the harmonium and played from memory both melody and accompaniment for her as best I could. Thereupon she became very friendly toward me and looked at me in a strange way. Still, she continued to pick out the chorale with one finger. Then it dawned upon me that I could do something she was unable to do, and I was ashamed of having shown off my skill, which I considered something quite natural. Usually, though, I was a quiet, dreamy pupil who did not learn to read and write without effort.

I remember one more thing from my first school year. Before I went to school, my father had already told me many Bible stories, among them the one about the Flood. Once when we had a very rainy summer, I assailed him, observing, "It has rained here about forty days and forty nights, yet the water has not even touched the houses, much less risen above the mountains." "Well, at that time," he answered, "in the beginning of the world, the rain didn't just come down in drops as it does now, it came down in bucketfuls." This explanation made sense to me.

Later, when the teacher at school told the story of the Flood, I waited for her to draw the distinction between the rain of that time and that of ours, but she didn't. At last I could no longer control myself. "Teacher," I called out from my seat, "you must tell the story correctly." Not allowing her to silence me, I continued, "You must say that at that time the rain did not come down in drops, but in bucketfuls."

When I was eight years old, my father gave me, at my request, a New Testament, which I read eagerly. One of the stories that occupied my mind most was that of the Wise Men from the East. What did Jesus' parents do with the gold and precious things they received from these men? I wondered how they could later have been poor again. It was completely incomprehensible to me that the Wise Men from the east never bothered about the Christ Child later on at all. I was also offended that there is no report about the shepherds of Bethlehem having become disciples of Jesus.

In my second year of school, we had lessons in penmanship twice a week with the teacher who gave singing lessons to the older children just before. Sometimes we came over from the elementary school too early and had to wait in front of the older children's classroom. When the two-part song "Down by the Mill I Was Sitting in Sweet Peace" or "Who Planted Thee, Oh Beautiful Forest?" began, I had to hold onto the wall to keep from falling down. The delight of the two-part music made my skin tingle and surged through my whole body. Also, when I heard brass music for the first time, I almost fainted. The violin did not sound beautiful to me, though, and I got used to it only little by little.

While at the village school, I witnessed the introduction of the bicycle. We had heard several times about the carters getting angry with people who dashed about on high wheels frightening the horses. Then one morning, as we were playing in the school yard during the break, we learned that a "speed runner" had stopped at the inn on the other side of the street. We forgot school and everything else and ran over to gape at the "high wheel" which had been left outside. Many grown-ups showed up as well and waited with us while the rider drank his pint of wine. At last he came out. Everybody laughed at the grown man wearing short pants. He mounted his bicycle and, lo, was gone.

In addition to the high wheels, the ones of medium height—the so-called kangaroos—were introduced in the mid-eighties. Soon thereafter the first low-wheeled bicycles appeared. The first bicyclists were taunted for not having the courage to get up on high wheels.

In my second to last year of high school, I myself acquired a bicycle, which I had fervently desired for a long time. It had taken me a year and a half to earn the money for it by tutoring students who lagged behind in mathematics. It was a second-hand bicycle which cost 230 marks. At that time, however, it was still considered unseemly for the son of a pastor to ride a bicycle. Fortunately, my father disregarded these prejudices. There was no shortage of those who found fault with the "arrogant" conduct of his son.

The well-known orientalist and theologian Eduard Reuss, in Strasbourg, did not want theology students to ride bicycles. When, as a student of theology, I moved into the St. Thomas Institute with my bicycle in 1893, the director, Erichson, remarked that he could permit this only because Professor Reuss was dead.

Today's youth cannot imagine what the coming of the bicycle meant to us. It opened up undreamed-of opportunities for getting out into nature. I used it abundantly and with delight.

I remember the first tomatoes just as I do the first bicycle. I may have been six years old when our neighbor Leopold brought us, as a great novelty, some of those red things which he had planted in his garden. The gift created some embarrassment for my mother, for she did not know how to prepare them. When the red sauce made its appearance on the table, it received such little appreciation that most of it went into the garbage. It was not until the end of the eighties that the tomato was generally accepted in Alsace.

My father's study was a very uncanny place to me. Only when I absolutely had to did I set foot in it. The smell of books that pervaded it took my breath away. It seemed terribly unnatural to me that my father was always sitting at the table, studying and writing. I could not understand how he could endure it and vowed to myself never to become a person like him who was forever studying and writing. I began to understand my father's literary efforts a little better when I was old enough to sense the charm of his village stories, which appeared in the Church Messenger and in calendars. His model was Jeremias Gotthelf, a Swiss pastor known for his writing. However, my father was more considerate; he avoided sketching the people who served as models for the characters in his stories so accurately that they could be identified.

Once a year, alas, I had to spend a day in my father's study. That was between Christmas and New Year's when Father declared after breakfast: "Today the letters are to be written! You accept the Christmas presents, but when the time for writing thank-you letters

The Schweitzer family, with Albert standing in the middle and his sisters Louise and Adele standing left and right. Margrete and Paul are sitting with their parents. Courtesy of Syracuse University Library.

comes, you are too lazy. So, get to work! And I don't want to see any sullen faces!"

Oh, those hours sitting with my sisters in the study, breathing the bookish air, hearing the scratching of my father's pen, while in my mind's eye I was with my friends gliding down the road behind the church on their sleds . . . and I had to write letters to uncles, aunts, godparents, and other givers of Christmas presents! And what kind of letters! In a life-time of writing I have never again faced anything as difficult as that. As a matter of course, all the letters had three parts and the same content:

1. Thanks for the present given by the addressee, accompanied by the assurance that it had afforded me the greatest pleasure of all my presents.

2. Enumeration of all gifts received.

3. New Year's wishes.

Although they all had the same content, each letter was supposed to be different from all the others! And in each letter I was faced with the enormous difficulty of finding a good transition from the Christmas presents to the New Year's wishes. I won't even mention the challenge of finding the courteous concluding phrase suitable to the addressee for each letter.

Each one had to be drafted and presented to my father. Then it had to be corrected, reworked and finally copied on a neat sheet of paper, without any mistakes or ink spots. Often it got to be time for lunch and I hadn't even roughed out one of the six or seven necessary letters.

For years I salted the meals between Christmas and New Year's with my tears! Once I even started crying right after receiving the presents on Christmas Day thinking of the letters that had now become unavoidable. My sister Louise managed to write each letter differently and to find ever new transitions from the presents to the good wishes for the New Year. No one has ever again impressed me as much as she did with her literary dexterity.

The disgust with studies and letter-writing which I acquired in my childhood because of these thank-you and New Year's letters remained with me for years. Although I have been forced by the conditions of my life to keep up an extraordinarily voluminous correspondence, I have still not learned to write letters which end nicely with New Year's wishes. Therefore, whenever I give Christmas presents as uncle or godfather, I always forbid the recipients to write me thank-you letters. They shall not salt their soup with tears as I used to at that time of the year. To this day I do not feel comfortable in my father's study.

The week after Christmas was the only one in which our father was strict with us. At all other times he allowed us as much freedom as children can handle. We appreciated his kindness and were deeply grateful for it. During summer vacations he took us to the mountains two or three times a week for whole days. Thus we grew up like wild roses.

In my third year of school, I was promoted to the school for older children where Father Iltis taught us. He was a very competent teacher. Without putting in much effort, I learned a lot from him.

Throughout my life I have been glad that I started my education in the village school. It was good for me to compete with the village boys and to discover that they were at least as clever as I. I never shared the arrogance shown by so many boys who start in the "gymnasium" and think that the children of the educated are by nature more gifted than those who walk about in patched pants and wooden shoes. Even today, when I run into my former classmates in the village or the fields, I immediately remember where their abilities exceeded mine. This one was better in mental arithmetic, that one made fewer mistakes in dictation, a third always knew the historical dates and still another was first in geography. One—I mean you, Fritz Schöppeler—had a better handwriting than the teacher himself. To this day I recall each one as superior to me in some subject.

At age nine I was sent to the secondary school in Münster. Mornings and evenings I had to walk three kilometers beside the hills. My delight was to walk alone, without the classmates who took the same route, and to indulge my thought. How deeply I experienced autumn, winter, spring, and summer in those years. When, during the vacation of 1885, it was decided that I should attend the gymnasium in Mulhouse in Upper Alsace, I cried secretly for hours. I felt that I would be cut off from nature.

I tried to put my enthusiasm for the beauty of nature as I experienced it on my walks to Münster into poems; but I never got beyond the first two or three rhymes. Several times I also tried to sketch the mountain with its old castle on the other side of the road. However, I also failed at that. From then on I resigned myself to enjoying beauty simply by looking at it without attempting to translate it into art. I never again tried to draw anything or render it in verse. Only in improvising music have I been creative.

At the secondary school in Münster it was Pastor Schäffer who taught religion. He was a distinguished religious personality and, in his way, an excellent speaker. The way he told the Bible stories took our breath away. I still remember how he cried at the teacher's desk and we sobbed on our benches as Joseph revealed himself to his brothers. He nicknamed me Isaak, which means "he who laughs," for I was easily provoked to laugh, a weakness which my classmates exploited mercilessly in school. Quite often the class register read: "Schweitzer laughs." Yet I was not cheerful, but rather shy and reserved.

I had inherited this reserved temperament from my mother. We lacked the gift of expressing in words the love we felt for each other. I can count on my fingers the times when we really had heart-to-heart talks, but we understood each other without words.

I also had inherited from my mother a deeply passionate nature, which she in turn had inherited from her father—who was very kind, but at the same time very irascible. I became aware of my passionate disposition when playing games. I took every game very seriously and got angry when others did not play with similar devotion. When I was nine or ten, I once struck my sister Adele because she played a game carelessly and let me win an easy victory. From that time on I became afraid of my passion and gradually gave up all games. I never dared touch a playing card. I also stopped smoking on January 1, 1899, because it had become an addiction.

I had to fight hard against my hot temper. I remember many events of my childhood which still humiliate me and keep me watchful in this struggle.

My grandfather Schillinger, who died before I was born, had been a zealous worker for enlightenment— a man quite filled with the spirit of the eighteenth century. After the service he used to inform his congregation, who waited for him outside, of the political news and also acquainted them with the latest discoveries of the human mind. When there was something special to see in the sky, he set up a telescope in front of his house in the evening and let everyone look through it.

Since the Catholic priest was also inspired by the spirit of the eighteenth century and its open-

mindedness, the two clergymen lived in brotherly harmony in their neighboring vicarages. If one of them
had more guests than he had space for, he would put
them up in the other's parsonage. If one of them went
on a trip, his colleague would occasionally visit the
sick of the other denomination so they would not lack
spiritual comfort. On Easter morning when the Catholic priest was hurrying from mass to his Easter meal,
my grandfather would open his window and call out
to him his congratulations on the end of Lent.

One night there was a great fire in the village.
When the Protestant vicarage seemed threatened, it
was evacuated and the contents stored in the Catholic
one. That was how my grandmother's hoop skirt came
to be in the priest's bedroom and had to be taken back
into the other parsonage the next morning.

My grandfather prepared his sermons meticulously.
On Saturdays his house had to be very quiet. No visitor
was admitted. When his son was a college student, he
even had to plan to arrive for vacation on some day
other than Saturday.

He seems to have been an autocrat, the good Pastor
Schillinger. He kept people in awe. If a person wanted
to talk to the pastor, he had to appear at the parsonage

in a black coat and a tall hat. Numerous anecdotes about him still make the rounds back in the valley.

Two of these deal with the "Turt," the classic meat pie of the Münster Valley. As pastor, he had to cut these at the wedding and baptismal meals over which he presided. Once he is said to have asked whether it mattered where he cut the pie. When he was told it did not matter, he said, "In that case I will cut it at home."

Another time he cut one piece too few by mistake. When the platter returned without a piece for him he said, "I don't like it that much anyway, you know," even though everybody knew how fond of it he was.

These and other stories about Pastor Schillinger are still told and still evoke the customary laughter at wedding and baptismal meals in our valley.

The parsonage in which he lived and the church in which he preached are no more. Bombs have shattered them. A big trench was cut through the middle of the church, but the old pastor's grave beside it remained intact as if by a miracle.

When I was still so small that I hardly understood what was said to me, my mother told me I was called Albert in memory of her late brother. This brother—

really a half-brother from the first marriage of my grandfather—had been the pastor of the Church of St. Nicolai in Strasbourg.

In 1870, after the Battle of Weissenburg, he was sent to Paris to get medical supplies in preparation for the expected siege of Strasbourg. There, instead of receiving the medicines urgently requested by the Strasbourg physicians, he was given the runaround. When he finally started home with a small portion of what had been requested, the fortress was already completely surrounded. General von Werder, the commander of the German besieging army, allowed the medical supplies to get through to Strasbourg, but made my uncle a prisoner of war. Living through the siege among the besiegers, he worried that his congregation would think he had left them in the lurch in those difficult times of his own free will. Because he had a heart ailment, he never got over the stress of those months. In the summer of 1872 he collapsed and died, surrounded by his friends, in Strasbourg.

The idea of continuing the existence of a person who had been so dear to my mother gave me a lot to think about, especially since I was told so much about his kindness. When for a while milk was very scarce after

Schweitzer, age ten, before entering the gymnasium in Mulhouse, Alsace. Courtesy of the Albert Schweitzer Center and Syracuse University Library.

the siege of Strasbourg, he took his milk to a poor old woman every morning. After his death, this woman told my mother how she had gotten her morning milk at that time.

As far back as I can remember, I have suffered because of the misery I saw in the world. I never really knew light-hearted youthful enjoyment of life, and I believe this is true of many children even though they seem quite cheerful and carefree.

What especially saddened me was that the poor animals had to suffer so much pain and misery. The sight of a limping old horse being dragged to the slaughterhouse in Colmar by one man while another beat it with a stick haunted me for weeks.

Already before I started school it seemed quite incomprehensible to me that my evening prayers were supposed to be limited to human beings. Therefore, when my mother had prayed with me and kissed me goodnight, I secretly added another prayer which I had made up myself for all living beings. It went like this: "Dear God, protect and bless all beings that breathe, keep all evil from them, and let them sleep in peace."

I had an experience during my seventh or eighth year which made a deep impression on me. Heinrich

Bräsch and I had made ourselves rubber band sling-
shots with which we could shoot small pebbles. One
spring Sunday during Lent he said to me, "Come on,
let's go up the Rebberg and shoot birds." I hated this
idea, but I did not contradict him for fear he might
laugh at me. We approached a leafless tree in which
birds, apparently unafraid of us, were singing sweetly
in the morning air. Crouching like an Indian hunter,
my friend put a pebble in his slingshot and took aim.
Obeying his look of command, I did the same with
terrible pangs of conscience and vowing to myself to
miss. At that very moment the church bells began to
ring out into the sunshine, mingling their chimes with
the song of the birds. It was the warning bell, half an
hour before the main bell ringing. For me, it was a
voice from Heaven. I put the slingshot aside, shooed
the birds away so that they were safe from my friend,
and ran home. Ever since then, when the bells of Pas-
siontide ring out into the sunshine and the naked trees,
I remember, deeply moved and grateful, how on that
day they rang into my heart the commandment "Thou
shalt not kill."

From that day on I have dared to free myself from
the fear of men, and when my innermost conviction

was at stake, I have considered the opinions of others less important than before. I began to overcome my fear of being laughed at by my classmates. The way in which the commandment not to kill and torture worked on me is the great experience of my childhood and youth. Next to it, all others pale.

Before I began attending school, we had a yellow dog named Phylax. Like many dogs, he could not stand uniforms and always attacked the mailman. Therefore, I was given the job of restraining Phylax when the mailman was due, for Phylax was apt to bite and had once assaulted a policeman. Wielding a switch, I used to drive Phylax into a corner of the yard and keep him there until the mailman had left. What a proud feeling it was to stand in front of the barking, snarling dog like a lion tamer and master him with blows when he wanted to break out of the corner! That proud feeling did not last, however. When we were later sitting together again as friends, I reproached myself for having beaten him. I knew I could keep him away from the mailman by holding his collar and stroking him. Nevertheless, when the critical hour approached, I yielded again to the intoxication of playing a tamer of wild beasts.

During vacations I was allowed to play the coach-man for our next-door neighbor. His brown horse was already somewhat old and short-winded. He was not supposed to trot much. Nevertheless, in my driver's passion I again and again let myself be carried away. I forced him into trotting even when I knew and felt that he was tired. The pride of controlling a trotting horse bewitched me. The neighbor allowed it "in order not to spoil my fun." What became of the fun, though, when I unharnessed the horse at home and saw how hard he was breathing, which I had not noticed from my seat on the wagon? What good was it to look into his tired eyes and ask him silently for forgiveness?

Once, when I was in high school and home for Christmas vacation, I drove a sleigh. The neighbor's dog, Löscher, who was known to be vicious, came out of the house and lunged, yelping, at the horse. I thought I was within my rights when I gave him a well-aimed blow with my whip, although it was clear that he was only attacking the sleigh playfully. Alas, I had aimed all too well. Hit in the eye, he howled and wallowed in the snow. His wailing haunted me. I could not free myself from it for weeks.

Twice I went fishing with other boys. Then, horrified by the maltreatment of the skewered worms and the tearing of the fishes' mouths, I did not go along with them any longer and even found the courage to prevent others from fishing.

From such experiences, which moved my heart and often put me to shame, there slowly arose in me the unshakable conviction that we may inflict death and suffering on another living being only when there is an inescapable necessity for it and that we must all feel the horror of thoughtlessly killing and causing pain. This conviction has driven me ever more powerfully. I have become more and more certain that in the depths of our hearts we all feel this. We do not dare admit it and act accordingly because we are afraid of being smiled at condescendingly by others who would consider us as "sentimental." We allow our feelings to be blunted. I, however, vowed to myself never to become emotionally blunted and never to fear the reproach of sentimentality.

In Mulhouse I stayed with Uncle Louis and Aunt Sophie, a childless old couple. Uncle Louis was a half-brother of my paternal grandfather, and my godfather. As such, he had offered to let me live in his house free of charge while I was a student at the gymnasium.

Thus he made it possible for my father to send me to school; otherwise he could not have afforded it. Only later did I appreciate the kindness that Uncle Louis and Aunt Sophie did me by taking me into their house. In the beginning I felt only the strict discipline to which I was subjected.

My uncle was the superintendent of the elementary schools of Mulhouse and lived in a somewhat gloomy official apartment in the Central School next to Maria-hilf Church. Earlier (around 1855, if I am not mistaken) he had lived for a fairly long time in Naples. There he had directed the Franco-German School, which the German and French colonies maintained jointly at that time.

Life at my great-uncle's house was regulated to the minutest detail. After lunch I had to practice the piano until it was time to go to school again. Once the school assignments had been completed in the evening, I had to go back to the piano. "You don't know how useful music will be to you later in life," my aunt would say when she had to chase me to the piano. She could surely not foresee that music would eventually help me earn the means for founding a hospital in the jungle.

Only Sunday afternoons were set aside for recreation. We went for walks, and afterwards I was allowed to satisfy my passion for reading until 10 o'clock in the evening. This passion was boundless. It is still with me today. I am unable to put down a book that I have started to read. I would rather spend all night on it, but at least I have to skim through it. If I like it, I promptly read it two or three times in a row.

My aunt abhorred this "devouring of books," as she called it. She also had a passion for reading, but in a different way. As a former teacher, she read, as she said, in order to enjoy the style, which is the essential thing. Every evening for three hours she pored over a book while knitting or crocheting; one hour before dinner, two afterwards. When the style was exceptionally beautiful, the needles slowed down, like horses when the coachman is negligent. Sometimes she exclaimed: "Oh, that Daudet! Oh, that Theuriet! What style! Oh, that Victor Hugo knows how to describe!" As she read Julius Stinde's *The Buchholtz Family,* the tears of laughter ran down her cheeks. Nevertheless, she would not spend an extra quarter of an hour on the book. At half past ten she placed the book mark and closed it.

So, as we sat at the same table with our different kinds of reading passion, each found the other to be enigmatic. Greatly concerned about my education, my aunt sought to slow down my tempo when once again I had finished a book too fast. She endeavored with kindness, with authority, and with sarcasm to break me of "sniffing" through books and to convert me to a reasonable pace. Nothing worked. No one can overcome his nature. Her arguments failed to move me because I am convinced that one can pay attention just as well when "devouring" a book, and indeed that one can best distinguish between good and bad writing that way. If, in a hurried reading, I succumbed to the temptation of skipping sentences, or even whole descriptions, I judged that the book was badly written. When, on the other hand, I was so fascinated that I could not help reading each sentence, I thought that the style had to be good. I still think so today. I was, however, careful not to share this wisdom of mine with my aunt because I wished to avoid irritating her on the subject. She had me completely in her power because she determined whether I was allowed to read a quarter of an hour more or less.

What was particularly distasteful to her was that I pounced on the newspapers. I had only a quarter of an hour available to read them—the time when the table was set for dinner forcing me to interrupt the work on my school assignments. Immediately I reached for the "Strasbourg Post," the "Mulhouse Daily," and the "New Mulhouse Times." My aunt wanted to forbid me reading the newspapers on the grounds that I was only looking at the serial novels and murder stories. However, I protested that I was particularly interested in politics, that is, in contemporary history.

I was then about eleven years old. The problem was referred to my uncle. During dinner he said, "We will see right away whether the boy really reads the political news." He began to examine me, asking me what princes occupied the thrones of the Balkan countries and what the names of their prime ministers were. Then I had to tell him the composition of the latest three French cabinets. Finally I had to recite for him the content of Eugen Richter's latest speech before the German Diet. Over fried potatoes and salad I passed this exam with flying colors. Thereupon the judgment was pronounced that I was allowed to read the newspapers not only as the table was being set but also after finishing my homework. Of course I also refreshed my soul with the novels in the literary supplement, but politics was really my main concern. From then on my uncle started to treat me as a grown-up and to discuss politics with me during meals.

I inherited my interest in public affairs from my mother. As an avid reader of newspapers, she was always dissatisfied that none were printed on the day after Christmas, on Easter Monday and on Whitsun Monday, although she was a pious woman and zealously defended holiday rest.

I have followed political events with keen interest since my ninth year and have experienced them consciously. My uncle's information about earlier times was very valuable to me.

There also lived in my uncle's house Miss Anna Schäffer, the daughter of the pastor of Münster. She was a teacher at the girls' high school. Through her wisdom and friendliness, she contributed more to my education than she ever suspected. I was also treated with much kindness in the house of my classmate Eduard Ostier. His mother was an outstanding woman. For a number of years, Ostier spent the Whitsuntide vacations with us in Günsbach.

I also often visited the house of Pastor Matthieu. His son, an unusual and important personality, attended school with me. Like me, he later studied the-

ology. He worked as a teacher of religion at the boys'
school in Zürich. Matthieu's father was extraordinarily
learned and well-read. With the exception of these two
families, I had no social contacts; my aunt was not in
favor of "gadding about."

In my first years at Mulhouse, I suffered greatly
from being cut off from nature. Once, on a sunny
March day when the last snow was melting, I looked
longingly out the window from the table at which I
was beginning to do my homework after the four
o'clock coffee break. My aunt, who was ironing, must
have sensed what was going on within me. I could not
believe my ears when I heard her say, "Come along, I
am going to take you for a walk." Over the bridge of
the canal on which ice blocks were still floating, we
went up the Rebberg. My aunt did not press for an
early return. Only when it was getting completely
dark did we go home. We did not talk much, but from
that day on my relationship to her changed. Now I
knew that the woman who brought me up so strictly,
sometimes with pedantic severity, had a heart and understood my longing.

When I was older, I was allowed to go for walks by
myself on free Wednesday and Saturday afternoons. I

always went to the hills, which enclose Mulhouse so beautifully on the south, and looked longingly toward the mountains in the vicinity of the Münster Valley. Often I met an old gentleman there who carried his hat in his hand and let his white hair flutter in the wind. I knew him because I had seen him in the pulpit. It was Adolf Stöber, the Alsatian poet, who was a pastor in Mulhouse. He used to take home a bunch of wild flowers. As time went on, he treated me as an acquaintance and let me accompany him a ways. This association with a real poet filled me with pride.

Mrs. Ostier, my school-mate's mother, had a large garden on the Rebberg. How many beautiful hours did I spend in that garden!

In my first year in Mulhouse, I was not a good student either. I was too much given to day-dreaming. My bad report cards caused my parents much sorrow, yet I did not find the energy to pull myself together and do better. I was in danger of losing the scholarship I had as a pastor's son. My father was summoned to see the principal, who hinted that it might be best if he took me out of the gymnasium. In my dreaminess I did not realize the worries I created for him! I was surprised that he did not scold me, but he was too kind and too sad for that.

At that juncture, a savior appeared in the person of a new home-room teacher. His name was Dr. Wehmann. In spite of my dreaminess, this much became clear to me in the first days of his teaching: this teacher had carefully prepared each class. He knew exactly how much ground he wanted to cover in it and always completed what he had planned. He always returned tests punctually on the due date and in the due hour. This self-discipline which I observed in him had an influence on me. I would have been ashamed to displease this teacher. He became my model. After three months, when we received our Easter report cards, I was already one of the better students, even though the Christmas report card had been so bad that my mother had walked about with her eyes red from tears during the whole Christmas vacation.

Later, when Dr. Wehmann was transferred to Thann and then to Saargemünd and Strasbourg, I again used to visit him. He knew how much I owed him. Upon my return from Africa at the end of World War I, he was one of the first people I tried to visit. I did not find him. Having contracted a nervous disease because of lack of food, he had taken his own life, I was told. Through him I gained an insight which I have tried to apply in my work as an educator: that a profound sense of duty pervading even the slightest detail is a great educational force which accomplishes what no exhortations or punishments can achieve.

Initially I did not please my music teacher, Eugen Münch, either. He was the organist of the Reformed St. Stephen's Church, who had just come from the Berlin Academy of Music. "Albert Schweitzer is my torment," he used to say. This was because, on the one hand, I played by sight and improvised instead of studying the assigned pieces during the practice hours forced upon me by my aunt; on the other hand, however, I was too shy to expose my feelings by playing in the presence of my teacher. I could not get myself to reveal to him what I experienced in a beautiful work of music. I imagine it is the same with many music students. Because of this I angered him with my "wooden playing."

Once, after I had, in my self-consciousness again rattled off a badly practiced Mozart sonata, he placed before me the short Mendelssohn-Bartholdy "Song

Without Words" in E-Major. In a bad mood he said, "Actually, you are not worthy of being given beautiful music to play. You will probably mess up this "Song Without Words," too. When a person has no feeling, I can't give him any either." "Oho," I thought, "I'll show you that I have feeling!" Throughout the next week I eagerly practiced this piece, which I had often played by sight; I even tried out the best fingerings, something nobody had ever succeeded in making me do before, and wrote them in. In the next lesson, when I had happily gotten beyond the scales and the prelude, I pulled myself together and played the "Song Without Words" the way I felt it in my heart. My teacher did not say much, but clapping me firmly on the shoulder, he played for me another "Song Without Words." Then I was assigned a piece by Beethoven. After a few more lessons, I was judged worthy to begin Bach. Still a few lessons later, I was allowed to take organ lessons on the beautiful instrument in St. Stephen's Church. That fulfilled one of my secret wishes, for I had always longed to play the organ. It was in my blood. My paternal grandfather, Pastor Schillinger of Mühlbach, had spent much time with the organ and organ playing. When he came into a city he did not know, the first thing he did was to look at the organs. When the famous organ in the collegiate church in Lucerne was being built, he traveled there and spent whole days in the choir loft to observe the construction and try out the masterpiece of the organ builder Haas. He is said to have improvised beautifully. My father, too, had that gift. As a child I listened to him for hours when he improvised at dusk on the old square piano which had come down to us from grandfather Schillinger. However, he never liked Bach's music.

Through the kindness of Father Iltis, and because he had need of a substitute, I had played the Günsbach church organ when I was but a boy. By the age of nine, I was taking his place during services. Now, at fifteen, I was privileged to learn the expert use of the pedals on an organ with three manuals and sixty-two stops from the great organist Eugen Münch. I could hardly believe my good fortune. At sixteen I was allowed to substitute for Eugen Münch in the services. Soon after that, I played the organ in concert for the first time.

My teacher was performing the Brahms *Requiem* with the choir of the church and entrusted to me the organ accompaniment. It was then that I experienced for the first time the delight of letting the sound of the organ surge into that of orchestra and choir, a pleasure which I have since tasted so often. Unfortunately, after Münch's death, the beautiful organ of St. Stephen's Church was destroyed and modernized in such a barbaric manner that it completely lost the wonderful tone it had at that time.

I was sent to old Pastor Wennagel for confirmation classes. I had great respect for him, but I did not open up to him. I was a diligent confirmation student, but the good pastor never had an inkling of what moved my heart. So many problems that occupied my mind were not solved by his teaching, even though it was quite solid. How many questions I would have liked to put to him! But one was not allowed to do that.

On one point, despite my respect for him, my thinking differed markedly from his. He wanted to make us understand that all reasoning had to give way to faith. I, however, was convinced, and still am, that it is precisely through reasoning that the fundamental ideas of Christianity have to be confirmed. Reason, I told myself, has been given to us so that we may grasp through it all thoughts, even the most sublime ones of religion. This certainty filled me with joy.

During the last weeks of instruction, Pastor Wennagel kept a few of us after each class to talk to us privately about the confirmation. When it was my turn, he questioned me kindly about the thoughts and resolutions with which I approached the holy hour. I began to stammer and answer evasively. Much as I liked him, it was impossible for me to let him look into my heart. The conversation ended sadly. I was coolly dismissed. Deeply concerned, Pastor Wennagel later told my aunt that I was going to my confirmation with indifference. The truth was, however, that during those weeks I was so moved by the holiness of the season that I almost felt ill. Confirmation was a great experience for me. When our group entered the church from the vestry on Palm Sunday, Eugen Münch was playing "Lift up Your Heads, Ye Gates" from Händel's Messiah. It was in wonderful harmony with the thoughts in my heart.

As a vicar at St. Nicolai in Strasbourg, I held confirmation classes for boys for about ten years. How often I had to think of dear Pastor Wennagel and myself when one of them seemed indifferent! Then I always told myself that much more goes on in a child's heart than it lets on. I tried to see to it that the boys in my classes could approach me with what troubled them. Twice a month an hour was allotted to questions that they might want to ask me.

In my first years in Mulhouse I suffered a lot of homesickness for the church in Günsbach. I missed my father's sermons and the services familiar to me since my childhood. These sermons made a great impression on me because I noticed how much of what my father said in the pulpit came out of his own experience. I became aware of how much effort—and even struggle —it was for him to lay open his heart every Sunday to the members of his congregation. I clearly remember today sermons of his that I heard while I was still attending the village school.

I liked the afternoon services most; I almost never missed one when I was in Günsbach. In these intimate devotions, my father's unpretentious way of preaching was at its best. The melancholy feeling that the festive day was approaching its end gave these services a peculiar solemnity.

From the services in which I participated as a child, I took with me into life a feeling for the solemn and the need for stillness and spiritual concentration. I cannot imagine my existence without this feeling. Therefore, I cannot agree with those who do not want

This sculpture, by Frédéric Bartholdi, the sculptor of the Statue of Liberty, representing Africa, is part of a monument in Colmar that includes the allegories of all continents. It made a deep impression on Schweitzer as a child and later as a student. "His face, with its sad thoughtful expression, spoke to me of the misery of the Dark Continent," he wrote. Courtesy of Syracuse University Library.

to let children take part in services for grown-ups because they cannot understand them. What matters is not understanding but experiencing the solemn. Seeing the adults in their devotion and being caught up in it is what is meaningful for the child.

My interest in missions also goes back to the afternoon services in Günsbach. On the first Sunday of every month, my father conducted a service dedicated to missions in which he spoke about the life and work of missionaries. On a series of Sundays, he once read to us the memoirs of Casalis, the missionary to the Bassutos, which he had translated from French for this purpose. They made a deep impression on me.

Next to Casalis, it was the sculptor Bartholdi from Colmar, the creator of the Statue of Liberty at the entrance to New York Harbor, which directed my young thoughts to faraway countries. On his monument of Admiral Bruat on the Champ-de-Mars at Colmar there is the sculpture of a Negro, carved in stone, no doubt one of the most impressive works his chisel created. It is a Herculean figure with a thoughtful, sad expression. This Negro gave me a great deal to think about. Whenever we went to Colmar, I sought an opportunity to look at him. His face told me about the misery of the dark continent. To this day, I make a pilgrimage to see him when I am in that town.

The church building in which the services were held also contributed to the nostalgia for Sundays in Günsbach which I experienced in Mulhouse. The beautiful new church there seemed terribly sober to me because it lacked a chancel. In Günsbach, however, the Catholic chancel allowed free rein to my devout dreaming, for that church was used by both Protestants and Catholics for their services.

When Alsace became French during the reign of Louis XIV, the king, intending to humiliate the Protestants, decreed that in Protestant villages in which there lived at least seven Catholic families, the chancel had to be made available to the Catholics. Every Sunday, the church was to be at their disposal for services at certain hours. That is why a number of Alsatian churches are both Protestant and Catholic at the same time. In the second half of the nineteenth century, their number decreased somewhat because some congregations decided to build separate churches for the Catholics. However, in Günsbach and elsewhere the practice of Protestants and Catholics using the same church survives to this day.

The Catholic chancel into which I used to gaze was, to my childlike imagination, the quintessence of magnificence. The altar was painted gold. It had huge bouquets of artificial flowers on it and tall metal candlesticks holding majestic candles. On the wall above the altar and between the two windows stood two big gilded statues. To me, these represented Joseph and the Virgin Mary. All this was flooded with the light which streamed in through the chancel windows, and through these one looked out on trees, roofs, clouds, and sky—on the world which continued the chancel of the church into infinity and which was steeped in the aura of transfiguration. Thus my gaze wandered from the finite into the infinite. Calm and peace filled my soul.

Because of these memories of my youth, I do not appreciate efforts to create a Protestant type of church building. When I see churches in which modern architects try to realize the ideal of a church just for sermons, my heart aches. A church is much more than a place where one listens to sermons. It is a place for devotion. In itself, as a space, it must be conducive to spiritual concentration. However, it cannot accomplish this if one's gaze collides with walls in all directions.

*Schweitzer, about seventeen years old, with his brother
and sisters at the parsonage in Günsbach.* Left to
right, *Albert, Paul, Margrete, unidentified girl,
Adele, and Louise. Courtesy of Syracuse University Library.*

The eye needs an inspiring distance to turn its outward vision inward. Therefore, the chancel is not something Catholic, but is part of the essence of a church. If the Protestant service is by nature sober, the church building must not also be so. It must complement the service with word, song, and prayer and become an experience of the soul.

From the church that is both Protestant and Catholic I have taken with me into life another idea: that of religious reconciliation. The church shared by Protestants and Catholics, though born of a royal whim of Louis XIV, is to me more than a peculiar historical phenomenon. It is a symbol of my conviction that denominational differences are destined to disappear in time. While still a child, I thought it beautiful that in our village both Protestants and Catholics celebrated their services in the same church. I am still filled with joy each time I set foot in it. I wish all Alsatian churches common to both denominations may stay that way as a prophecy pointing towards the future of religious unity for which we must strive if we are truly Christians. The differences which arise out of the joint ownership of the church can be overcome with a little good will on both sides, as experience has shown in Alsace.

It is true, however, that if two hot-headed shepherds of souls have to share the House of God, their common tenancy may not make for harmony but rather for strife. Once on a Whitsun Monday in the eighteenth century, a Protestant minister in Lower Alsace gave his sermon while the Catholic priest read mass. They had not been able to agree on the time each would use the church.

The altar whose golden splendor I once admired is no more. Upon the initiative of a Catholic priest from Münster who was a connoisseur of art, it had to give way to a stylish high altar. Mary and Joseph would have been covered up; so they no longer stand bathed in light between the chancel windows. Their place is now between its sidewalls. Instead of standing next to each other looking down into the church and blessing the congregation, they stand on opposite sides, gazing at each other. Mary no longer gleams in noble golden splendor, but has had to clothe herself in red, green, and blue in accordance with the style forced upon her.

Now when I sit in the Günsbach church, I close my eyes to see the chancel's simple magnificence which once delighted me. As my imagination lingers on the past, figures appear who were once in the church in the flesh but are no longer there because they have been carried out into the churchyard. The memory of the dead who once worshiped with us is to me the most moving experience when I now attend services in my hometown church. How they sat there, the men all in black, the women in the simple traditional dress of the Münster Valley! How much more solemn were they in dress, comportment and character than are we —the new generation!

One old man named Mitschi was so deaf he could not understand a word of the sermon. Nevertheless, every Sunday he was sitting in his place. Once, when my father commiserated with him because he had to take part in the service without being able to hear anything, he shook his head with a smile and said, "The community of the saints, pastor, the community of the saints."

After I had given up my daydreaming, thanks to Dr. Wehmann, I remained a good student, but I did not always sit among the best. I really only had a true gift for history. In languages and mathematics I achieved only in accordance with the effort I expended. History, however, I mastered without effort. My passion for reading, which over time had concentrated on historical works, was of great value to me. I was lucky in that Professor Kaufmann, who taught history, was a great scholar in his field. In the upper grades, he treated me more as a friend than a pupil. I remained in contact with him until his death.

Next to history, it was the classes in nature study which fascinated me most. In that field we had a very effective teacher, Dr. Förster. He was, it is true, not at all outstanding in physics and chemistry. His specialty was geology. Once he was granted a leave of absence to carry out geological research in Sumatra, if I am not mistaken. When he derived formulas in chemistry or physics on the blackboard, it was obvious that he had just learned them for that class. However, that did not diminish his authority at all. His teaching was good because it was well prepared. Unfortunately the number of natural science classes at the gymnasium was then much too small.

The instruction in nature studies held something strangely exciting for me. I could not escape the feeling that we were not told sufficiently how little is really understood of what is going on in nature. I had a downright hatred for the natural science textbooks. Their confident explanations formulated for memorization—which, I noticed, were already somewhat out-dated—did not satisfy me in any way. It seemed ridiculous to me that wind, snow, hail, rain, the formation of clouds, the spontaneous ignition of hay, the trade winds, the Gulf Stream, thunder, and lightning were supposed to have been explained. For me a special enigma was the formation of the rain drop, the snowflake, and the hailstone. It wounded me that the ultimate mysteriousness of nature was not recognized and teachers confidently claimed to have an explanation where only a more deeply penetrating description had been achieved; this made the mysterious only more mysterious. Already then it had become evident to me that what we call "force" and "life" remains forever inexplicable to us in its essence.

Thus I drifted into dreaming about the thousand wonders that surround us. Fortunately it did not keep me from my school work as the earlier thoughtless dreaming had. I still dream that way today, and this dreaming is growing ever more overpowering. When I sit at the dinner table and see the light broken into rainbow colors in a water jug, I am capable of forgetting everything around me. I cannot free myself from the spectacle.

Love of history and of natural science went hand in hand for me. Gradually I recognized that historical events too are full of enigmas and that we must forever give up the idea of really understanding the past. In history, too, we are only able to give a more or less penetrating description.

Throughout my school years, I found the lessons in which poems were dissected unbearable. I experienced as ugly and senseless the attempt of making me sensitive to a poem by explaining it. Talking about it only served to destroy the emotion the work of the poet had awakened in me. There is nothing about a poem that needs to be explained; one has to experience it. Thinking this way made me a very inattentive—even rebellious—pupil in these classes. Instead of following the lesson, I read passages here and there in the textbook and became inebriated, without guidance, with the poems and readings which particularly attracted me. I felt that I had closed the windows to protect myself from the street noises.

Homer left me cold. He was altogether spoiled for us because we were supposed to know who the parents, grandparents, aunts, cousins, gods, and goddesses of the heroes were. Genealogies and kinships have never been my thing.

From my fourteenth to my sixteenth year, I went through a disagreeable phase of development. I became insufferable to everyone, especially to my father, because of my contentiousness. I wanted to engage everybody I came across in thorough and rational discussions concerning the questions which were in the wind at the time. I wanted to uncover the errors of conventional opinions and to help establish the correct views. The joy of seeking the True and the Useful had come over me like an intoxication. Every conversation I participated in must needs get to the very bottom of things. Thus I shed my previous reservedness and became a troublemaker in conversations that were supposed to be nothing but casual. How many table conversations in Mulhouse and Günsbach did I derail onto disastrous tracks! My aunt called me impertinent because I argued with adults as if they were of my own age. When we went to visit somebody, I had to promise my father not to spoil his day with "stupid behavior" in conversations.

As a matter of fact, I was as unbearable as a half-way

decently bred young person can possibly be. It was not mere contentiousness, however, that made me behave that way. Rather it was a passionate need to think and to seek with others the True and the Useful. Grandfather Schillinger's spirit of enlightenment had awakened within me. The conviction that the progress of mankind consists of replacing mere opinions and thoughtlessness by reason had taken possession of me and showed itself at first in a stormy and disagreeable manner.

After this bad fermentation, the wine cleared. At bottom I have remained what I was then. However, now I do my best to combine it with the decent behavior expected in polite society in order not to be a nuisance to others. I resign myself to taking part in conversations and to unthinking chatter without rebelling. My innate reserve has helped me to acquire again this behavior of a well-bred person.

Yet, how often I rebel inwardly! How I suffer from spending so much time unprofitably with others instead of talking seriously about serious matters and opening ourselves to one another as striving, suffering, hoping, and believing human beings!

Often I think it downright immoral to wear a mask.

Many a time I ask myself to what extent one may display good breeding without sacrificing one's truthfulness. If I meet people with whom I may enter into disputes as a thinking person, I enjoy them passionately as if I were as young as I was then; and if a serious young debater crosses my path, I engage in cheerful fencing with him in which the difference in age, for better or for worse, does not matter.

During my years at the gymnasium, it was Director Wilhelm Deecke who made the most profound impression on me. He came to Mulhouse when I was moving into the upper grades. A native of Lübeck, his somewhat stiff behavior at first struck us as alien, but we soon got used to it.

Deecke was an excellent pedagogue, a universally educated philologist, and a profound human being. We sensed that he did not only want to impart knowledge to us, but to make real human beings of us. We were vaguely aware that he had incurred the displeasure of the governor, General von Manteuffel, by candidly expressing his views and that he had had to pay for this with a demotion. His position at the Mulhouse gymnasium really amounted to banishment. We were filled with admiration for him because despite this he was always cheerful and gave his all in the lessons, though he must have had much higher ideas on his mind. He was for us a modern Stoic. We especially respected him because he was friends with the poet Geibel, the historian Mommsen, and other famous people and because he was regarded as an authority on ancient Greek inscriptions and in Etruscan studies. He spiced up his lessons by opening vistas on all sorts of subjects and problems that were in some way connected with the subject under discussion. Unforgettable for me are the hours in which he read Plato with us and thereby acquainted us with philosophy in general. His favorite philosopher was Arthur Schopenhauer. A short time after we had left the gymnasium, when the authorities were about to do him justice, he died of stomach cancer.

For a prolonged period of time a shadow lay over my otherwise sunny youth. There were financial worries in the parsonage with the five children. My mother economized wherever she could. I made it a matter of pride to need as little as possible in Mulhouse. Once in the fall, my mother said my winter suit must have become too small for me and I would need a new one. I denied it, but since I really could not wear it anymore, I went about all winter in my yellow summer suit. My aunt did not object, for she was in favor of making me tough; but being considered a have-not by my classmates offended my boyish vanity. I endured it only to lessen my mother's worries.

As my mother told me later, she cooked with shortening instead of with butter. In the eighties this was not manufactured as well as it was later and often had a disagreeable aftertaste. My mother attributed the stomach ailment which my father contracted at that time to the use of shortening. Rheumatism of the joints, which he caught in a humid bed in Strasbourg, got him down even further. Thus our family lived through sad weeks and months. I will forever remember that time when my mother's eyes were always red with tears.

At the time of my confirmation my father's health began to improve. One reason for this was that at that time we exchanged the old parsonage, which was somewhat damp and enclosed by other buildings, for a new one looking out on a sunny garden. This house, an old building into which we moved at the end of the eighties, had been remodeled by Mr. Adolph Müller, the son of a former Günsbach pastor. When he retired from his engineering career and moved back to his native village, he had made it very livable and serviceable. Upon his death he left it to the parish for use as a parsonage. During the war, its basement—built with massive walls dating back to the the middle of the nineteenth century—served the whole neighborhood as a bomb shelter.

With increasing age my father became again more and more vigorous. As a septuagenarian during the war, he took care of his congregation under the fire of the enemy guns. Even now, in his high seventies, he still works as a pastor, completing almost fifty years of service in Günsbach. During the war, my mother was run over by army horses and killed on the way to Weier-in-the-Valley.

As time went on, we were relieved of the most burdensome financial worries. A distant childless relative of my mother's, a Mrs. Fabian from Wasselnheim, left us her small fortune. Thus during my later high school years, the sun shone again over my home.

We were all in good health and lived together in the most beautiful harmony. The relationships between parents and children were ideal thanks to the great understanding our parents had for us in all things, even in our follies. They brought us up in the spirit of freedom. Since I had given up my distasteful passion for disputes, there never was a trace of that tension between the father and the adult son which disturbs the happiness of so many families. My father was my dearest friend.

We thought it was especially kind of our parents that they allowed us to bring school friends home with us for vacations until the house was full. How my mother managed to cope with the work we caused her this way has remained a puzzle to me to this day.

The thought that I was privileged to enjoy such a singularly happy youth was on my mind all the time. It downright oppressed me. More and more insistently the question arose in me whether I could accept my good fortune as a matter of course.

Thus wrestling with the problem of whether we have a right to good fortune became the second great experience of my life. The other one, which had accompanied me since my childhood, was that of being deeply stirred by the suffering in the world around us. These two experiences slowly became interwoven. They determined my view of life and my future.

It became ever clearer to me that I did not have the

right to accept as a matter of course my happy youth, my good health, and my capacity for work. From the deepest feeling of happiness, there slowly grew within me the understanding of the word of Jesus that we must not live our lives for ourselves alone. Whoever has been spared personal suffering must feel called upon to help alleviate the suffering of others. We must all share in the burden of pain that oppresses the world.

Darkly and confusedly that thought was working on me. Sometimes it let go of me, permitting a breath of relief and the thought that I would again become complete master of my life. However, a small cloud had risen on the horizon. From time to time I could look away; but it was growing slowly and irresistibly. In the end it covered the whole sky.

The decision was made when I was twenty-one. A student home for the Whitsuntide vacation, it was then that I decided I would devote my life to preaching, scholarship, and music until I was thirty; thereafter, when I had achieved what I planned in scholarship and music, I would start on the road of direct service to humankind. What that road would be, I expected circumstances to reveal to me as time went on.

Dedicating myself to medical service in the colonies was not my first decision. That idea occurred to me after I had considered plans of different kinds of humanitarian service which I had had to give up for various reasons. A chain of circumstances then showed me the way to those who suffered from sleeping sickness and leprosy in Africa.

When in 1893, at the age of eighteen, I was preparing for the final examination at the gymnasium, I sensed only darkly that thoughts were thinking themselves within me to which I would have to submit later on. The claims of the immediate future asserted themselves. I was looking forward to my student days. Boldly I determined to take up theology, philosophy, and music at the same time. My good health, which tolerated the necessary night study, enabled me to carry out this intention. However, it was much harder than I had foreseen.

I passed my final examination at the gymnasium satisfactorily, but not as well as I had expected. The reason was the trousers I wore that day. I owned a black frock coat, which I had inherited from an old relative of my mother's, but no black trousers. In order to save, I did not want to have any made, so I asked

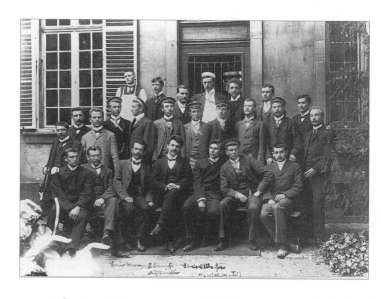

Schweitzer (first row, center) *in his twenties with the students of the Collegium Wilhelmitanum, Strasbourg. Courtesy of Syracuse University Library.*

my uncle to allow me to take the exam in his trousers. He was much shorter than I and portly while I was gangling and slender at that time; but we thought it would do for this one occasion.

Unfortunately I had neglected to try on the trousers. When I donned them on the morning of the exam, they hardly came down to my shoes even though I had lengthened the suspenders with string. A white gap yawned at the upper edge of the trousers. I refrain from describing how they fitted in back.

My appearance provoked unrestrained mirth among my fellow examinees. I was turned around and inspected from all sides. Our solemn entrance into the examination room was bungled because we could not suppress our laughter. When the teachers at the examination table saw my trousers, they were also quite amused. However, the stern school superintendent from Strasbourg (his name was Albrecht), who presided over the examination, did not notice what was going on. He saw only that I was the reason for the untimely merriment and made a severe remark on our irreverent behavior in general and about me in particular. Intending to drive the insolence out of the supposed clown, he undertook to examine me himself in all subjects except in mathematics, in which he was admittedly completely ignorant. He gave me a hard time. Encouraged by friendly glances from the principal, I stood my ground as best I could, but I was unable to answer a number of the questions the stern examiner asked and saw him shake his head many times.

He was particularly indignant because I could not tell him how the ships of the Greeks were beached according to Homer. When the other candidates did not know much more about that than I did, he criticized this as an unforgivable lack of education. I, however, considered it a much greater lack of education that we left the gymnasium without knowing anything about astronomy and geology.

Finally the superintendent examined me in history, which was his specialty. After ten minutes he seemed to be a different person. His anger had melted away. He no longer examined me but conversed with me about the difference between the Greek and Roman colonial enterprises.

In the final address, after the announcement of the examination results, he once more mentioned what pleasure it had been for him to examine me in history.

A compliment to that effect, proposed by him, adorns my otherwise very mediocre graduation certificate. Thus everything ended pleasantly.

It was very hard for me to take leave of my uncle and aunt. They still lived for a number of years, and I was able to show them how fond I was of them. When my uncle gave up his position in Mulhouse because of age, they moved to Strasbourg. There they rest in the churchyard of St. Gall, where my uncle Schillinger, the preacher at St. Nicolai, is also buried.

When I look back at my youth, I am moved by the thought of how many people I have to thank for what they were to me and what they gave me. At the same time, however, I become depressed when I realize how little I have expressed my gratitude to those people when I was young. How many of them said farewell to life without my having told them what their kindness or patience had meant to me. Deeply moved I sometimes softly spoke at their graves the words that I should have said to them while they were living.

Yet I think I can say that I was not ungrateful. Early on I woke up out of the youthful thoughtlessness of accepting as a matter of course their kindness and patience. I believe I became aware of that as early as I did of the suffering in the world. Yet, up to my twentieth year, and even beyond that, I did not try sufficiently to express the gratitude that I felt. I realized too late what it means to people to actually receive expressions of gratitude. Often it was also shyness which prevented me from showing my thankfulness.

Since I have myself had this experience, I don't think that there is as much ingratitude in the world as is usually asserted. I have never been able to interpret the story of the ten lepers as if only one of them was grateful. However, nine of them first went home to quickly greet their loved ones and look after their affairs and intended to go to Jesus immediately afterwards to give him thanks. Only things turned out otherwise. They were detained longer than they had anticipated, and meanwhile Jesus died. One of them, however, had the gift of spontaneously following his feelings. He sought out the person who had helped him and refreshed him with his gratitude.

Thus we must all exert ourselves to follow our impulses and allow our inner thankfulness to find expression. Then there will be in the world more sunshine and more strength to do good. Every one of us, however, must fight against making the bitter word about the ingratitude in the world part of his life view. Much water flows underground which does not gush forth as a spring. We may be consoled by this thought but we ourselves must be water that finds its way to become a spring at which people can quench their thirst for gratitude.

Another thought moves me when I think back of my youth: that so many people gave me something or were something to me without being aware of it. Some with whom I had never exchanged a word, some even whom I had only heard mentioned have had a definite influence on me. They entered my life and became forces within me. Much that I would not have sensed so clearly or done with such determination otherwise I feel and do because I am as if under the compulsion of those people. Therefore I believe that we all live spiritually of what others gave us in significant moments of our lives. These significant moments do not announce themselves but come unexpectedly. They also do not make a show of themselves but appear inconspicuous. Sometimes they even acquire their significance only in our memory, just as the beauty of a work of music or of a landscape reveals itself only in memory. Much of what has become our own in gentleness, kindness, ability to forgive, truthfulness, faithfulness, submission in suffering we owe to people in whom we experienced these qualities, whether in an important or unimportant event. A thought turned life lept into us like a spark and kindled a flame within us.

I do not think that one can put into a person thoughts which are not in him. Ordinarily all good thoughts are innate in people as tinder. Much of this tinder catches fire or catches it successfully only when it meets some flame or spark from outside, that is, from another human being.

Sometimes it may also happen that our own light is about to go out and is brought back to life again by what we experience in another person.

Thus each of us must think in great gratitude of those who have kindled flames within him. If those who have become a blessing to us were present with us and if we could tell them how they did, they would be surprised of what flowed from their lives into ours.

So no one knows how he affects others and what he gives them. That is hidden from us and must remain so. Sometimes we are allowed to see a little of it in order not to lose courage. The working of this power is mysterious.

Is there not altogether much more mystery in the relationship of man to man than we usually admit? None of us may assert that he really knows another person, even if he has lived with him day by day for years. Of what constitutes our experience we can communicate only fragments to even our closest friends. All of it we can neither express nor would they be able to grasp. We walk with each other in semidarkness in which no one can make out clearly the features of the other. Only from time to time, through an experience which we share with our companion or through a remark dropped between us, he stands for a moment next to us as if illumined by lightning. Then we see him as he really is. Afterwards we walk again next to each other in darkness, perhaps for a long time, trying in vain to imagine his features.

We have to accept the fact that each of us is an enigma to others. To know each other does not mean to know everything about each other, but to love and trust and believe in each other. One must not want to intrude into another person's inner being. Analyzing others—except in order to help mentally confused people—is ignoble. There is not only a bodily, but also a spiritual modesty, which we have to respect. The soul, too, has its cloak, which one should not tear off. None of us must say to another person: because we belong together in such and such a way, I have the right to know all your thoughts. Not even a mother may behave this way toward her child. All demands of this kind are foolish and harmful. In these relationships there can be only giving that elicits giving. Share of your spiritual being as much as you can with those who walk with you on your way and accept as something precious what comes back to you from them.

It was perhaps a consequence of my inherited reserve that the respect for the spiritual being of another person has been a matter of course for me since my youth. Later I was more and more confirmed in this view because I saw how much pain and sorrow comes from people's pretension to read in the soul of others like in a book that they own, and from the desire to know and understand in what respect they can and should believe in the other. We all must take care not to reproach our loved ones with lack of trust when they don't let us look at all times into the nicks and crannies of their hearts. It is indeed almost as if the more intimately we know each other, the more mysterious we become to each other. Only he who has respect for the spiritual being of others can really be something to them.

Therefore, I believe that no one should force himself to reveal more of his inner life than is natural to him. We cannot do more than allow others to get an inkling of our spiritual being and to sense theirs. The only thing that matters is to strive that there be light within us. One feels the striving in another human being, and where there is light in a person, it shines forth from him. Then we know each other, walking with each other in the dark without needing to probe the other's face and to reach into his heart.

Although the respect for the spiritual being of others has been natural to me since my youth, I have, on the other hand, had great trouble deciding how reserved we should be in the interaction with other people and how freely we may reveal ourselves to them. The two tendencies have fought within me. Until my last school years reservedness won out. My shyness prevented me from showing people as much sympathy as I felt for them and from offering them as much

Schweitzer with patients and staff at Lambaréné.
Photograph by Erica Anderson. Courtesy of the Albert
Schweitzer Center and Syracuse University Library.

service and help as I felt impelled to. In this attitude I was encouraged by the way my aunt in Mulhouse brought me up. She impressed on me reservedness as the quintessence of good breeding. I was supposed to learn to look upon any kind of "forwardness" as one of the greatest faults, and I endeavored to live up to this view. As time went on, however, I dared emancipate myself somewhat from the rules of reservedness and good breeding. They appeared to me like laws of harmony, which, it is true, are valid in general but are nevertheless often swept away by the living flow of music. I grasped more and more how many good things we miss when we allow ourselves to be slavishly locked into the reservedness which common politeness imposes on us.

On the other hand, we must surely strive to be tactful toward each other and not to meddle uninvited in other people's business. At the same time we have to remain conscious of the danger that lies in the reservedness which is demanded by daily life. It must not happen that we allow ourselves to behave like total strangers when facing an unknown person.

No man is ever a total and permanent stranger to any other man. Man belongs to man. Man has claims on man. Significant and insignificant circumstances may arise that overcome the distance at which we have to keep ourselves in daily life and bring us into a relationship with one another as human beings. The law of reserve is destined to be broken by the right to express feeling openly. Thus we all find occasion to step out of our reservedness and to become human beings to other human beings. Too often we miss these occasions because the current views about good breeding, politeness, and tact have robbed us of our spontaneity. Thus we deny another person what we would like to give him and what he is longing for. There is much coldness among people because we don't dare show ourselves as warm-hearted as we really are.

In my youth I had the good fortune of meeting some people who had retained their naturalness even though they observed the accepted forms of behavior in society. When I saw what they gave people by being the way they were, I found the courage to try to be as natural and warm as I felt myself. The resulting experiences never again permitted me to bow to the law of reserve. I now do the best I can to combine politeness of the heart with conventional politeness. I don't know whether I always manage. I can no more set up rules in this area than I can for music. When should one bow to the laws of harmony and when may one be guided by the spirit of music which is above all laws? My experience is that disregarding customary rules when directed to by one's heart and reflection, is seldom seen by others as thoughtless obtrusiveness.

The ideas which determine the essence and the life of a person are innate in a mysterious way. When we leave our childhood behind they begin to bud in us. When we are stirred by youthful enthusiasm for the true and the good, they blossom and begin to bear fruit. In our subsequent development the only thing that matters is how much of the fruit that started to grow on our tree of life in the spring reaches maturity.

The conviction that we have to struggle to remain as alive in our thinking and feeling as we were in our youth has accompanied me through life as a faithful mentor. Instinctively I have fought against becoming what is usually called a "mature person."

The word *mature* applied to human beings was, and still is, somewhat uncanny to me. I hear within it, like musical discords, the words impoverishment, stunted growth, and blunted feelings. What is usually considered maturity in a person is really resigned reasonableness. It is acquired by adopting others as models and by abandoning one after another the thoughts and convictions that were dear to us in our youth. We believed in the good; we no longer do so. We were zealous for justice; we are so no longer. We had faith in the power of kindness and peaceableness; we have it no longer. We could be filled with enthusiasm; we can no longer be. In order to navigate more safely through the dangers and storms of life, we lightened our boat. We threw overboard goods that we thought were dispensable; but it was our food and water that we got rid of. Now we travel more lightly, but we are starving.

In my youth I listened to conversations of grown-ups which wafted to me a breath of melancholy, depressing my heart. My elders looked back at the idealism and enthusiasm of their youth as something precious that they should have held on to. At the same time, however, they considered it sort of a law of nature that one cannot do that. This talk aroused in me the fear that I, too, would look back upon myself with such nostalgia. I decided never to submit to this tragic reasonableness. What I promised myself in almost boyish defiance I have tried to carry out.

Adults take too much pleasure in the sad duty of

preparing the young for a future in which they will regard as illusion all that inspires their hearts and minds now. Deeper life experience, however, talks differently to the inexperienced. It entreats the young to hold on to the ideas that fill them with enthusiasm throughout their lives. In the idealism of his youth, man has a vision of the truth. In it he possesses a treasure which he must not exchange for anything.

We must all be prepared for the sad fact that life is intent on robbing us of our faith in the good and the true, and our enthusiasm for it. But we don't have to make this sacrifice to life. When ideals collide with reality, they are usually crushed by facts. That, however, does not mean that ideals have to capitulate before facts to begin with. It only means that our ideals are not strong enough. They are not strong enough because they are not sufficiently pure, firm, and stable within us.

The power of ideals is incalculable. One does not see the power in a drop of water, but when it gets into a crevice and turns to ice, it splits the rock. Turned to steam, it drives the piston of a powerful machine. Something has happened to it which activates the latent force in it. So it is with ideals. Ideals are thoughts.

Dr. Schweitzer holding a baby just after it was born in the hospital at Lambaréné. Photograph by Erica Anderson. Courtesy of the Albert Schweitzer Center and Syracuse University Library.

As long as they are merely thoughts, the power that is in them remains ineffective, even if they are thought with the greatest enthusiasm and the firmest conviction. The power becomes effective only when they are thought by a noble human being.

The maturity to which we are called means becoming ever simpler, ever more truthful, ever purer, ever more peaceful, ever gentler, ever kinder, ever more compassionate. We do not have to surrender to any other limitation of our idealism. Thus the soft iron of youthful idealism hardens into the steel of adult idealism which will never be lost.

The great wisdom lies in overcoming disappointments. All reality derives from spiritual power; what is successful flows from power that is strong enough; what is not successful stems from power that is not sufficiently great. If my love is ineffective, it is because there is still too little love in me. If I am powerless against the untruthfulness and lies which thrive around me, it is because I am not truthful enough myself. If I must witness that malevolence and ill will keep playing their evil games, it is because I have not cleansed myself completely of pettiness and envy. If my peaceableness is misunderstood and ridiculed, it is because there is not enough peaceableness within me yet.

The great secret is to go through life as one who is not burned out. This is possible for those who do not count on other people or facts but are always thrown back on themselves in all experiences and look for the ultimate reason for everything in themselves.

Those who work on their inner perfection can never be robbed of their idealism. They experience the power of the good and the true within themselves. If they see too little success in their efforts to apply their ideals to the world, they know that they are only as effective as their inner perfection allows. Either the success has not come yet or it remains hidden from their eyes. Where there is power, there is effect of power. No ray of sunlight is ever lost but the green which it awakens needs time to sprout; and it is not always granted to the sower to live to see the harvest. All worthwhile work is done in faith.

So the knowledge about life which we grown-ups must impart to the young is not: "Reality will surely do away with your ideals" but rather: "Grow into your ideals so life cannot take them away from you." If people were to become what they are at age fourteen, how very different the world would be!

As one who tries to remain youthful in his thinking and feeling, I have wrestled with facts and experience for the sake of my belief in the good and the true. In our time, when violence clad in lies is sitting on the throne of the world, sinister as never before, I nevertheless remain convinced that truth, love, peaceableness, gentleness, and kindness are the powers above all powers. They will inherit the world if only enough people think and live thoughts of love, truth, peaceableness and gentleness with sufficient purity of heart and steadfastness.

All ordinary force limits itself, for it calls forth a counterforce which sooner or later becomes equal or superior to it. Kindness, however, works simply and steadily. It produces no tensions which impair it. It relaxes existing tensions; it makes mistrust and misunderstandings vanish; it grows stronger, calling forth more kindness. That is why it is the most practical and intensive force.

The kindness that a person radiates into the world works on the hearts and thoughts of men. It is our foolish failure that we do not dare practice kindness in earnest. We want to move a great load without availing ourselves of the lever that increases our power a hundredfold.

There is an immeasurably profound truth in these fantastic words of Jesus: "Blessed are the meek for they shall inherit the earth."

Kurt Bergel is a professor emeritus of history at Chapman University and the co-director of its Albert Schweitzer Institute. Born in Germany, he immigrated to the United States in 1940 and has taught at various universities and colleges in California. His association with Albert Schweitzer began in the early 1940s and continued until Schweitzer's death in 1965. He is the author of books and essays and, with Alice R. Bergel, edited and translated the correspondence between Schweitzer and the harpsichordist Alice Ehlers.

Alice R. Bergel, born in Berlin, took her Ph.D. in romance philology and philosophy at the University of Berlin. She taught foreign languages and philosophy at various colleges and universities. All her life she has worked for the better and more widespread knowledge of Schweitzer's life and thought through teaching college courses and giving talks in churches, clubs, and schools on Schweitzer. She now assists her husband, Kurt Bergel, at the Albert Schweitzer Institute.